Learning English level 1

Vocabulary activities for kids

ARTHWR BASS

Digital Creative Publishing

Author and Editor
Arthwr Bass

Colaborator
Sandra Lozada

Design and layout
Digital Creative Publishing

Publisher
Digital Creative Publishing

Photographs and illustrations
Digital Creative Publishing
Royalty Free Images (FFCU images)
Created by Freepik, www.freepik.com
(Credits to the respective author in each image)

© Arthwr Bass, 2019
digitalcreativepublishing@gmail.com

This book is intended for beginner students of the English language.
All rights reserved. The total or partial reproduction of this work is not allowed, nor its incorporation into a computer system, or its transmission in any form or by any means (electronic, mechanical, photocopy, recording, others) without previous and written authorization of the owners of the copyright. Infringement of these rights may constitute an offense against intellectual property.

Table of Contents

GREETINGS AND FAREWELLS 4
EMOTIONS 10
IN THE CLASSROOM 16
COLORS 24
FRUITS AND VEGETABLES 30
NUMBERS 36
SHAPES 42
FARM ANIMALS 48
SOURCES 53

Greetings and farewells

Read.

Every conversation, whether formal or informal, starts with a greeting. A greeting is something friendly or polite that people say when they meet someone. A farewell is something people say to wish happiness or safety when leaving.

Look at the pictures and Read.

Some formal greetings are good morning, good afternoon, and good evening. Informal greetings include hello and hi.
Good night is only used to say "good bye" during the night.

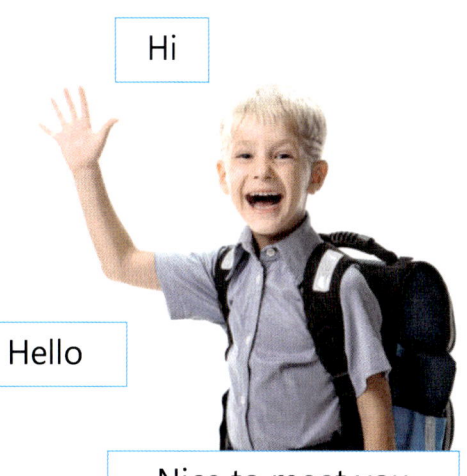

Good morning

Good afternoon

Good evening

Good night

Hi

Hello

Nice to meet you

Good bye

Bye bye

See you tomorrow

Take care

See you later

See you soon

Fill in the missing letters of the words.

Read and mark in the square (✓) if it is correct or (✗) if not. If it is incorrect, write it down in the correct way.

MO_N_NG
AF_ERN_ON
EV_NING
NIG_T
H_LLO
NIC_
B_E
H_
ME_T
LATE_
T_KE
TO_ORROW
SOO_
GO_D
S_E
C_RE
GRE_TINGS
FAREW_LLS

Good mourninight — *Good morning* ✗

Good evenight
_____

Bye, see you later
_____

Hello, nice to meet bye
_____

Good afternoon
_____

Hi, good bye
_____

Good afterning
_____

6

Solve the puzzle and find the mystery word.

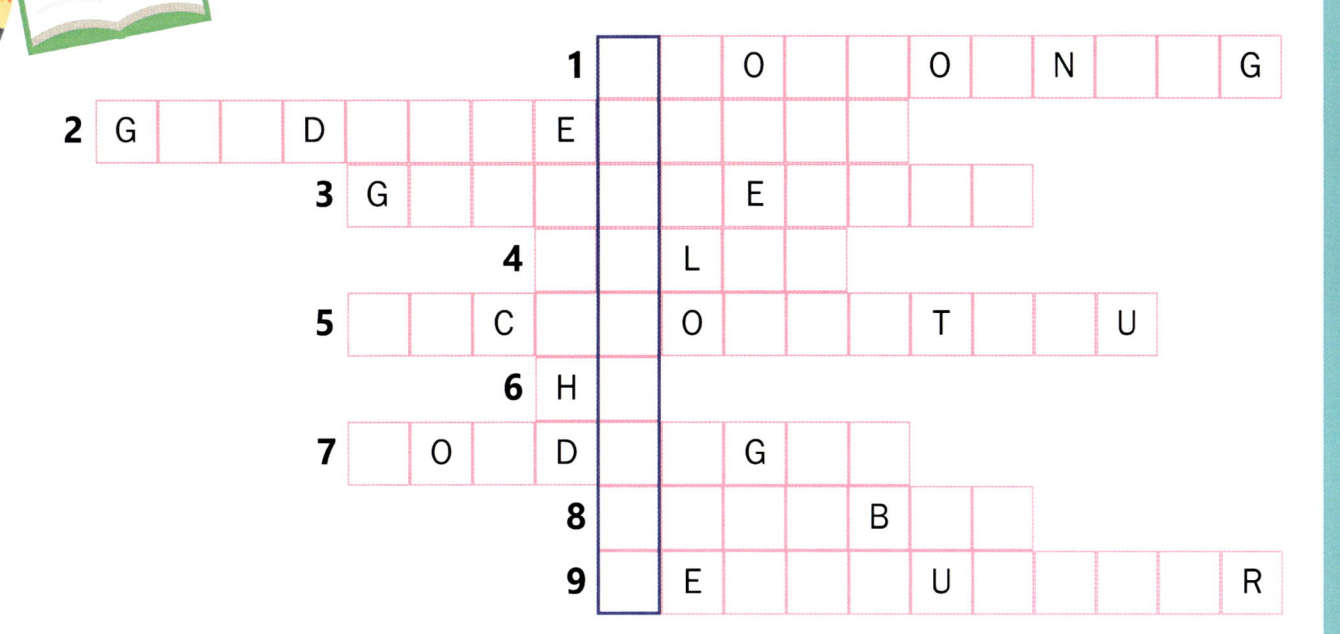

						1		O			O	N		G
2	G		D			E								
		3	G				E							
			4			L								
	5		C		O			T		U				
			6	H										
7		O		D		G								
			8				B							
			9	E			U			R				

1. A greeting you say when you meet someone in the morning.
2. A greeting you say when you meet someone in the afternoon.
3. A greeting you say when you meet someone in the night.
4. A simple way to greet someone also used to answer the phone.
5. A greeting when is your first time being introduced to someone.
6. The shortest greeting.
7. A farewell in the evening.
8. A farewell when someone is leaving and you wish them good.
9. A farewell when someone is leaving and who you expect to see later.

Circle the correct word that fills the blank and write.

Good _morning_
(morning)   night

Good _____
bye   afternoon

Good _____
evening   morning

7

Look at the pictures and read.

Hello! My name is Thomas

Hi! I am Jake

Hi! I am Diana

Hello! My name is Natalie

Hello! My name is Sophie

Hello! My name is Felix

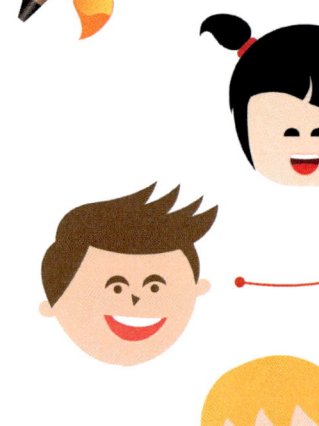

Match the pictures with the correct name.

Felix

Diana

Thomas

Sophie

Jake

Natalie

Read and write your name and the name of your best friend.

Hi! I am the new student. My name is _____. What is your name?

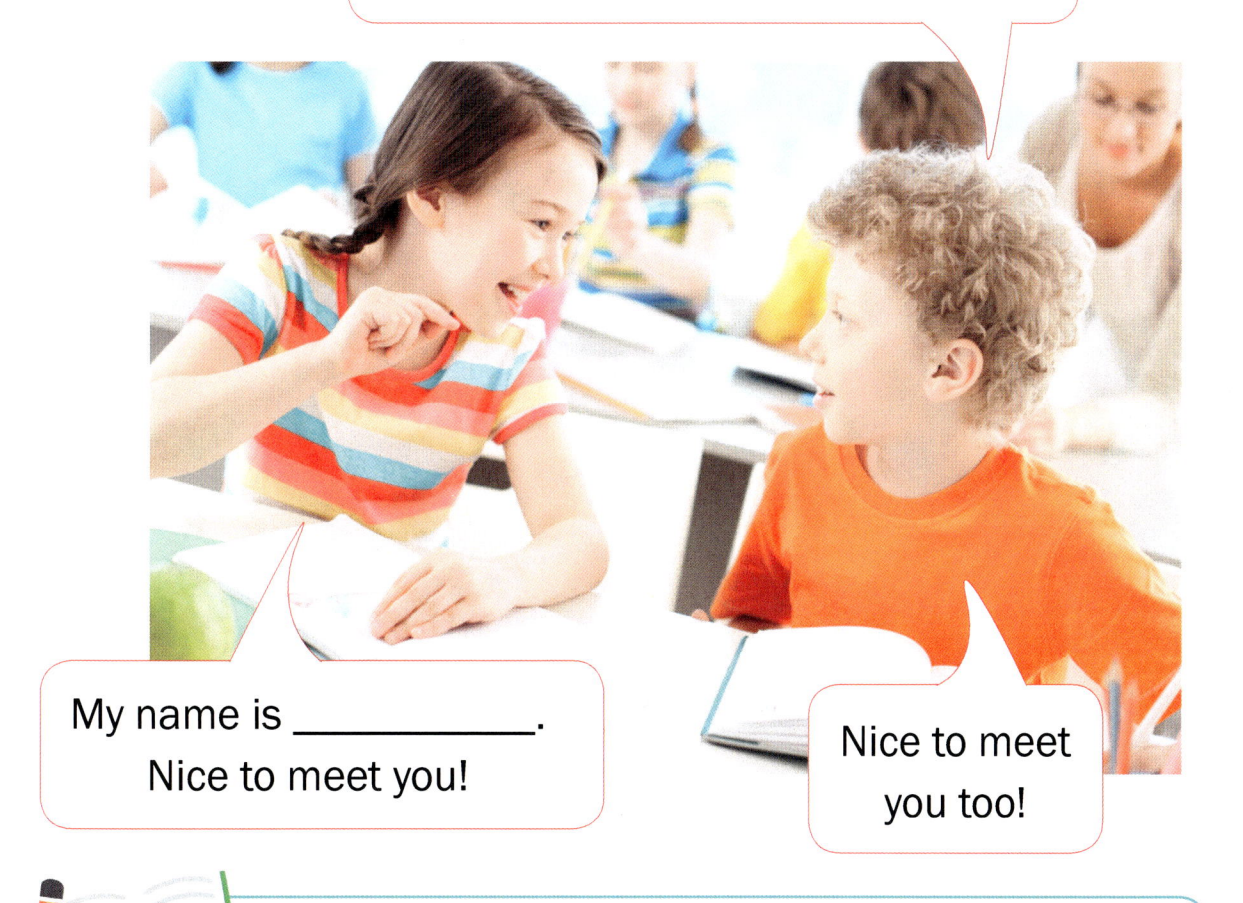

My name is _____. Nice to meet you!

Nice to meet you too!

Number the sentences to organize the conversation.

☐ Diana: Good morning Laura. My name is Diana.

☐ Laura: Let's be friends!

☐ Diana: Nice to meet you too! This is my first day too!

[1] Laura: Good morning. This is my first day at school. My name is Laura. What is your name?

☐ Laura: Nice to meet you Diana.

Emotions

Read.

Hi, Eli. How are you?

I am sad.

Why are you sad?

Because I lost my favorite doll.

I'm really sorry Eli.

Circle the correct word that fills the blank and write.

Her name is

_____

Sophia
Lesli
Eli
Daphne

She is

_____

Happy
Sad
Excited
Fine

Solve the puzzle by looking at the pictures of the emotions.

Happy

Sad

Shy

Embarrassed

Silly

Worried

Surprised

Angry

Excited

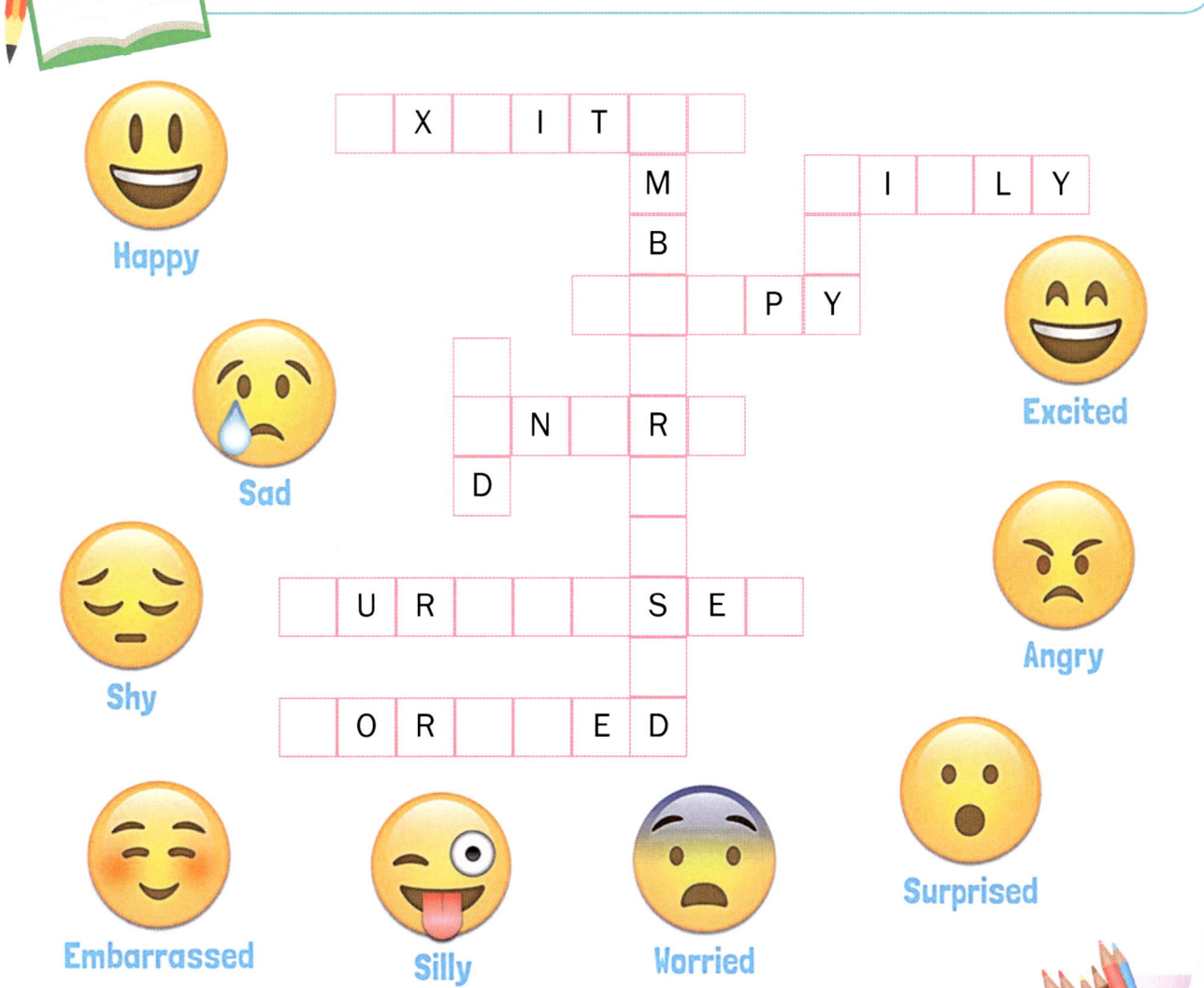

X I T
M   I L Y
B
P Y
N   R
D
U R   S E
O R   E D

Read and act every emotion with your friends.

Bored

Fine

Sad

Excited

Surprised

Shy

Angry

Worried

Embarrassed

Happy

Sick

Depressed

Silly

Confused

In love

Find the emotions from the list in the wordsquare.

Bored
Fine
Shy
Sad
Excited
Surprised
Embarrassed
Jealous
Happy
Angry
Worried
Silly
Confused
Sick
Lonely
Depressed
In love

A	B	O	R	E	D	K	L	E	J
F	G	D	S	G	H	E	S	M	W
I	T	A	S	H	Y	X	U	B	J
N	T	W	S	A	D	C	R	A	E
E	J	H	N	P	W	I	P	R	A
V	L	K	S	P	H	T	R	R	L
A	N	G	R	Y	J	E	I	A	O
W	O	R	R	I	E	D	S	S	U
W	A	G	V	N	B	W	E	S	S
S	I	L	L	Y	X	H	D	E	Z
I	C	O	N	F	U	S	E	D	S
C	P	N	O	I	U	Y	H	Q	X
K	D	E	P	R	E	S	S	E	D
I	N	L	O	V	E	X	S	D	F
B	G	Y	H	J	U	Y	T	R	E

Match the pictures with the correct emotion.

Happy
Sad
Fine
Angry
Bored
Worried

13

Look at the pictures and answer the question How Are you?

I am sick.
_____

_____

_____

_____

_____

_____

Hello!
My name is Lou.
I am happy.
How are you?

Draw the faces according to the emotion.

I'm happy. 　　　I'm worried. 　　　I'm sad.

I'm scared. 　　　I'm depressed. 　　　I'm angry.

Circle the correct emotion.

Angry
(Fine)
Bored
Worried

Sad
Shy
Angry
Excited

Happy
Worried
Angry
Shy

Sad
Angry
In love
Scared

Worried
Bored
Happy
Sad

In love
Shy
Angry
Sad

15

In the classroom

Read and memorize the classroom vocabulary.

Teacher

Student

Board

Notebook

Book

Pen

Pencil

Bag

Desk

Chair

16

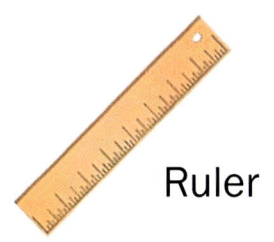

Ruler

Scissors

Eraser

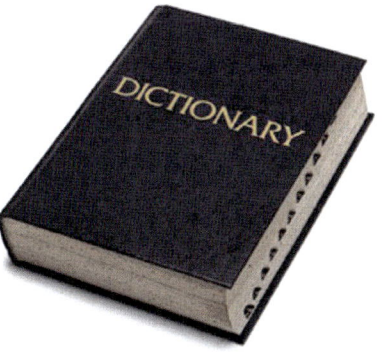

Dictionary

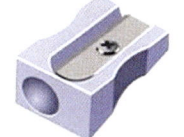

Pencil sharpener

Colored pencils

Garbage can

Computer

Write all the classroom elements you see in the picture.

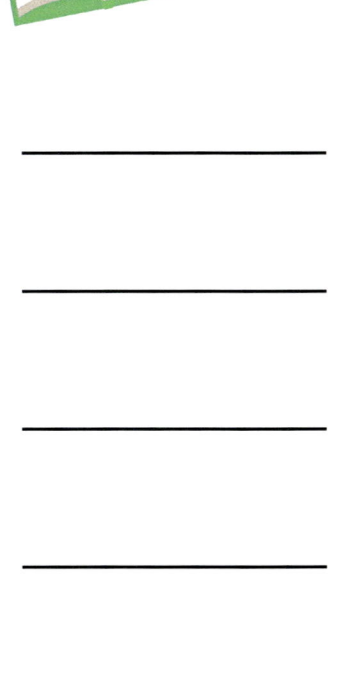

_____

_____

_____

_____

_____

17

Solve the puzzle and find the mystery word.

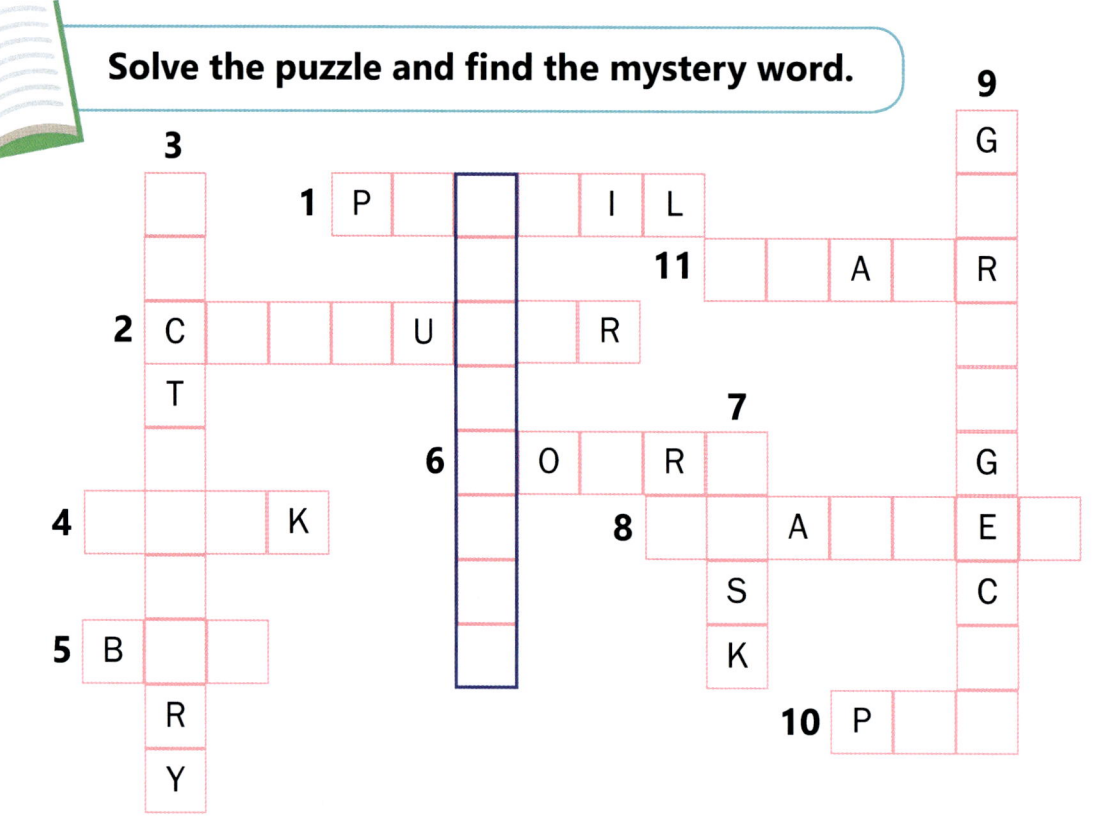

1. Implement for writing or drawing with a solid graphite core.
2. Electronic device to make processes, calculations and operations with data.
3. Book with a collection of words arranged alphabetically.
4. Pieces of paper with words printed on them fastened inside a cover.
5. Container used to hold all the school implements as books and pencils.
6. Big reusable writing surface on which text or drawings are made.
7. Piece of furniture used to write, draw, read and doing other school activities.
8. A person who teaches and helps others to acquire knowledge.
9. Where to put the garbage.
10. Writing instrument with tint.
11. Piece of furniture with a raised surface, commonly used to seat.

Fill in the missing letters of the words.

CO_P_TE_

_OA_D

D_SK

TE_C_E_

DI_TI_NA_Y

PE_CIL

NOT_BOO_

BA_

CHA_R

BO_K

G_R_AGE C_N

ST_D_NT

P_N

R_LER

ER_S_R

18

Write the classroom elements.

_____

_____

_____

_____

_____

_____

Read and draw in the square if the word is correct (✓) or incorrect (✗). If it is incorrect, write down the correct way.

| Compoutter | ✗ | Garbace gan | ☐ | Pensil | ☐ |
| Computer | | _____ | | _____ | |

| Dictionnari | ☐ | Student | ☐ | Desk | ☐ |
| _____ | | _____ | | _____ | |

| Notebook | ☐ | Teachert | ☐ | Chair | ☐ |
| _____ | | _____ | | _____ | |

Read the cards and memorize the classroom commands.

Be quiet

Raise your hand

Sit down

Stand up

Close the door

Make a line

Write

Read

Listen

Look at the board

Open the book

Close the book

Stop

Paint

Share

21

Fill in the missing letters of the sentences.

Write all the associated commands with the picture.

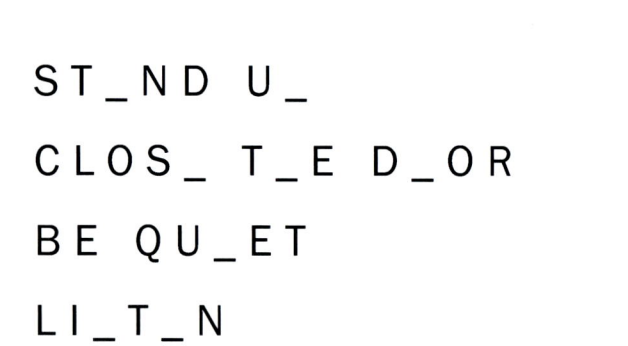

ST_ND U_

CLOS_ T_E D_OR

BE QU_ET

LI_T_N

W_IT_

REA_

O_EN T_E BOO_

LO_K AT TH_ B_AR_

CLO__ THE B_O_

SI_ DOW_

M_K_ A _INE

ST_P

P__NT

SH_RE

R_IS_ YOU_ H_ND

CL_SS_OO_

SC_OO_

Stand up

Sit down

22

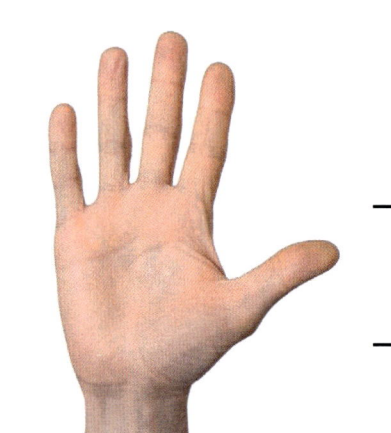

Find the classroom commands in the wordsquare.

A	F	G	H	B	R	E	R	W	L	I	S	T	E	N
C	L	O	S	E	T	H	E	D	O	O	R	W	R	C
L	M	N	R	Q	X	C	A	V	O	J	H	Y	T	L
S	T	O	P	U	Z	V	D	B	K	M	M	K	O	O
K	J	Y	T	I	N	W	V	N	A	A	I	O	P	S
S	S	W	E	E	P	A	I	N	T	K	W	E	E	E
H	T	N	M	T	V	C	X	Z	T	E	T	R	N	T
R	A	I	S	E	Y	O	U	R	H	A	N	D	T	H
T	N	R	I	I	S	H	A	R	E	L	B	N	H	E
I	D	Y	T	J	F	E	G	F	B	I	M	L	E	B
O	U	U	D	D	E	D	F	D	O	N	H	D	B	O
U	P	O	O	S	W	F	S	D	A	E	G	F	O	O
E	I	O	W	R	I	T	E	W	R	G	D	S	O	K
P	O	L	N	Z	L	X	G	H	D	H	S	S	K	L

Write the classroom command the teacher would say.

Be quiet

_____

_____

_____

23

Colors

Read and paint to discover the secondary colors.

Colors can be divided into primary, secondary and tertiary. Primary colors are the original parents of all the future generations of colors because when they are mixed they produce the secondary colors. Primary colors are unmixed pigments that can't be created by mixing other colors

PRIMARY COLORS

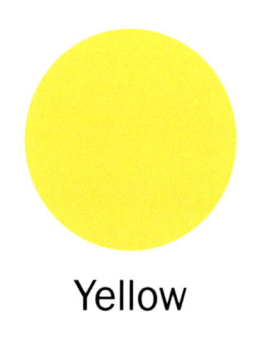

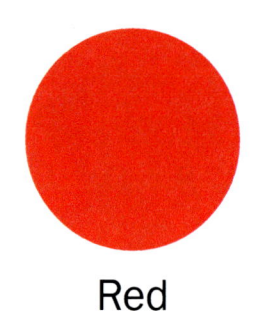

Yellow   Blue   Red

SECONDARY COLORS

⬤ + ⬤ = ⭕

⬤ + ⬤ = ⭕

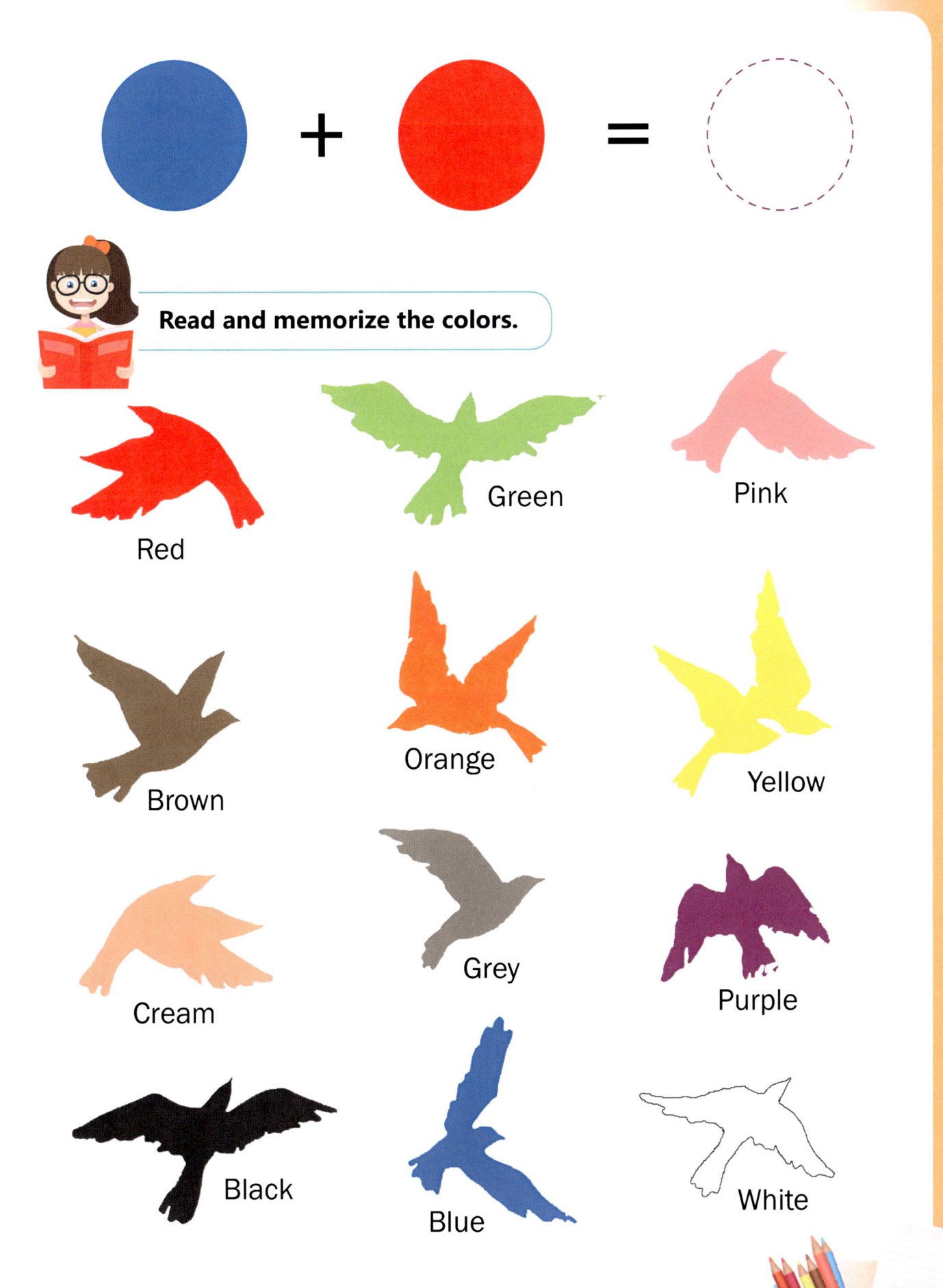

Read and memorize the colors.

Red

Green

Pink

Brown

Orange

Yellow

Cream

Grey

Purple

Black

Blue

White

Read and associate the colors with the objects.

RED

BLUE

YELLOW

PINK

GREEN

BROWN

ORANGE

26

Paint the stars with the indicated colors.

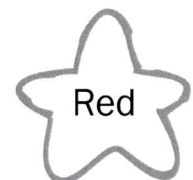

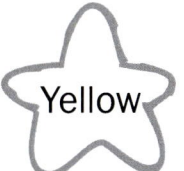

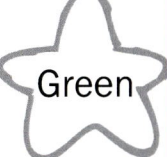

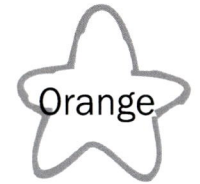

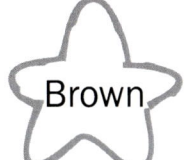

Red Yellow Green

Orange Brown Cream

Grey Pink Black

Find the colors in the wordsquare.

Orange
Yellow
Red
Green
Pink
Brown
Cream
Grey
Purple
Black
Blue
White

G	H	J	K	L	P	O	I	U	R
Q	W	R	W	B	L	A	C	K	W
C	Y	E	L	L	O	W	B	F	E
C	V	D	A	D	R	L	R	U	P
R	B	N	M	F	A	K	O	J	U
E	J	H	P	I	N	K	W	Y	R
A	K	Y	G	J	G	J	N	N	P
M	L	G	R	E	E	N	K	L	L
M	A	N	E	C	K	B	L	U	E
V	B	A	Y	Q	W	H	I	T	E

Fill in the missing letters of the colors.

R E _

B L _ E

O R _ N G _

G R E _

P I N _

P _ R _ LE

G R E _ N

Y E L _ O _

B R _ _ N

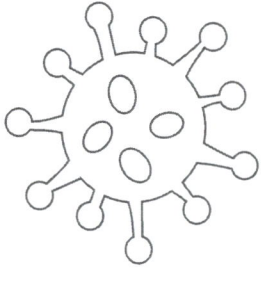

W H _ T _

C _ E _ M

B L A _ K

Paint the drawing with the indicated colors.

1. Red
2. Yellow
3. Green
4. Brown
5. Black
6. Cream
7. Orange
8. White
9. Pink

Fruits and vegetables

Read and memorize the fruits and vegetables.

Apple

Banana

Tangerine

Orange

Lemon

Grape

Kiwi

Coconut

30

Strawberry	Pear	Peach
Cherry	Raspberry	Blackberry
Tomatoe	Watermelon	Pineapple
Broccoli	Lettuce	
Cucumber		
Carrot	Spinach	

31

Fill in the missing letters of the fruits and vegetables.

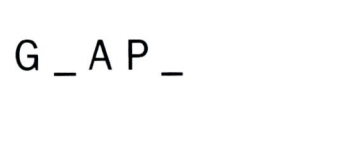

OR_N_E

STRA_B_R_Y

B_NA_A

BRO_CO_I

C_ER_Y

PE_R

AP_L_

C_R_O_

T_MA_O_

G_AP_

PI_E_P_LE

Write the fruit and the color according to the picture.

The _Apple_ is _Red_    The _____ is  _____   The _____ is _____

The _____ is  _____   The _____ is  _____   The _____ is _____

The _____ is  _____   The _____ is  _____   The _____ is _____

33

Find the fruits and vegetables in the wordsquare.

N	M	B	H	G	V	F	D	S	E	T	R	W	A	C	A	B	A	G
F	H	C	U	C	U	M	B	E	R	L	G	X	C	A	V	R	D	S
D	A	S	H	W	J	I	K	L	O	E	P	E	A	R	T	O	H	W
Y	G	P	R	A	P	P	L	E	C	T	E	A	V	R	R	C	W	A
T	R	I	T	T	U	K	L	P	O	T	A	C	V	O	Q	C	M	T
T	A	N	G	E	R	I	N	E	C	U	C	I	W	T	Z	O	L	E
O	P	A	L	R	I	W	Y	Q	O	C	H	E	R	R	Y	L	P	R
M	E	C	P	M	H	I	D	D	N	E	R	O	P	I	U	I	P	M
A	M	H	L	E	M	O	N	C	U	P	I	N	E	A	P	P	L	E
T	N	J	L	L	Q	Z	S	S	T	R	A	W	B	E	R	R	Y	L
O	V	W	P	O	R	A	N	G	E	U	R	T	U	E	F	D	J	O
E	H	B	A	N	A	N	A	P	R	A	S	P	B	E	R	R	Y	N
B	L	A	C	K	B	E	R	R	Y	Q	W	Y	T	R	I	U	R	T

Match the fruit with the color.

BANANA

APPLE

PEAR

LEMON

TANGERINE

ORANGE

STRAWBERRY

PINEAPPLE

WATERMELON

GRAPE

KIWI

CHERRY

Read and mark in the square (✓) if the word is correct or (✗) if it is incorrect. If it is incorrect, write it down in the correct way.

Wattermellon ✗
Watermelon

Banamena ☐
_____

Cranberry ☐
_____

Pineapple ☐
_____

Tangerine ☐
_____

Granpe ☐
_____

Rasberry ☐
_____

Grape ☐
_____

Blackperry ☐
_____

Paint the fruits and vegetables as you wish.

35

Numbers

Read.

1	2	3	4	5
One	Two	Three	Four	Five

6	7	8	9	10
Six	Seven	Eight	Nine	Ten

11	12	13	14	15
Eleven	Twelve	Thirteen	Fourteen	Fifteen

16	17	18	19	20
Sixteen	Seventeen	Eighteen	Nineteen	Twenty

Counting in tens, numbers always end in "ty". For example: 20 twenty, 30 thirty, 40 forty, 50 fifty, 60 sixty, 70 seventy, 80 eighty, 90 ninety. Double digit numbers, from 20, combine the vocabulary from counting in tens for the first digit and from 1 to 10 for the second digit. For example: 21 twenty one, 22 twenty two...

Count the fruits and write the number.

Three

Circle the correct number.

Five
Six
One
Four

One
Five
Six
(Three)

Seven
One
Nine
Four

Six
Four
One
Two

One
Six
Two
Three

One
Nine
Two
Six

Nine
Two
One
Seven

Two
Three
Six
Four

Count the fish and write the number.

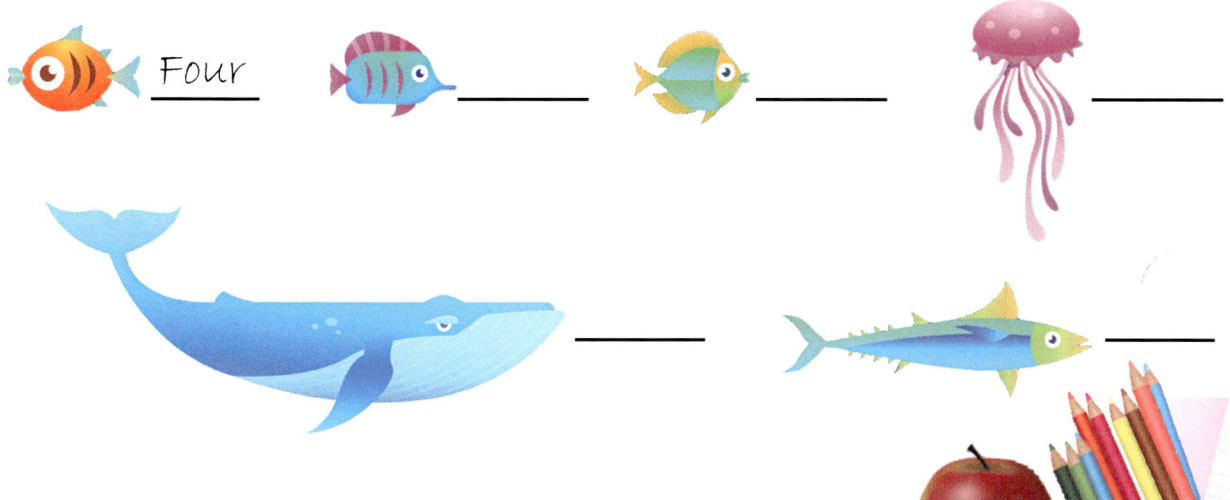

🐠 Four   🐟 ____   🐟 ____   🪼 ____

🐋 ____   🐟 ____

Count and write.

Six
_____   _____   _____

_____   _____   _____

Circle the group of fruits as indicated.

FOUR   FIVE   FOUR

THREE   TWO

Shapes

Look at the shapes and read.

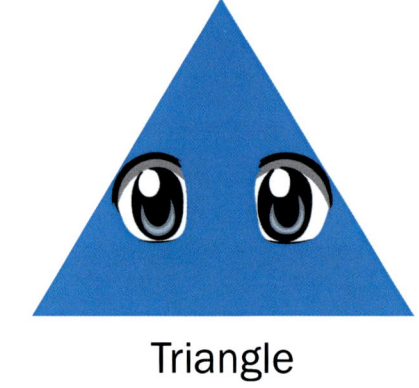

Circle

Triangle

Square

Star

Rectangle

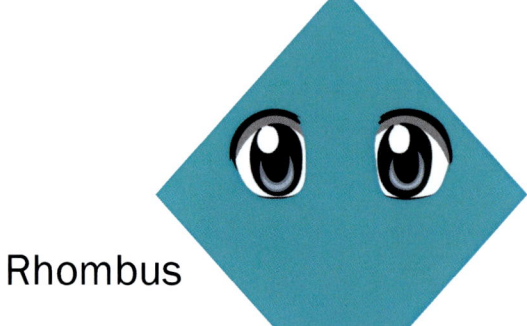

Heart

Rhombus

42

Follow and trace the path to the name of the shape.

RECTANGLE

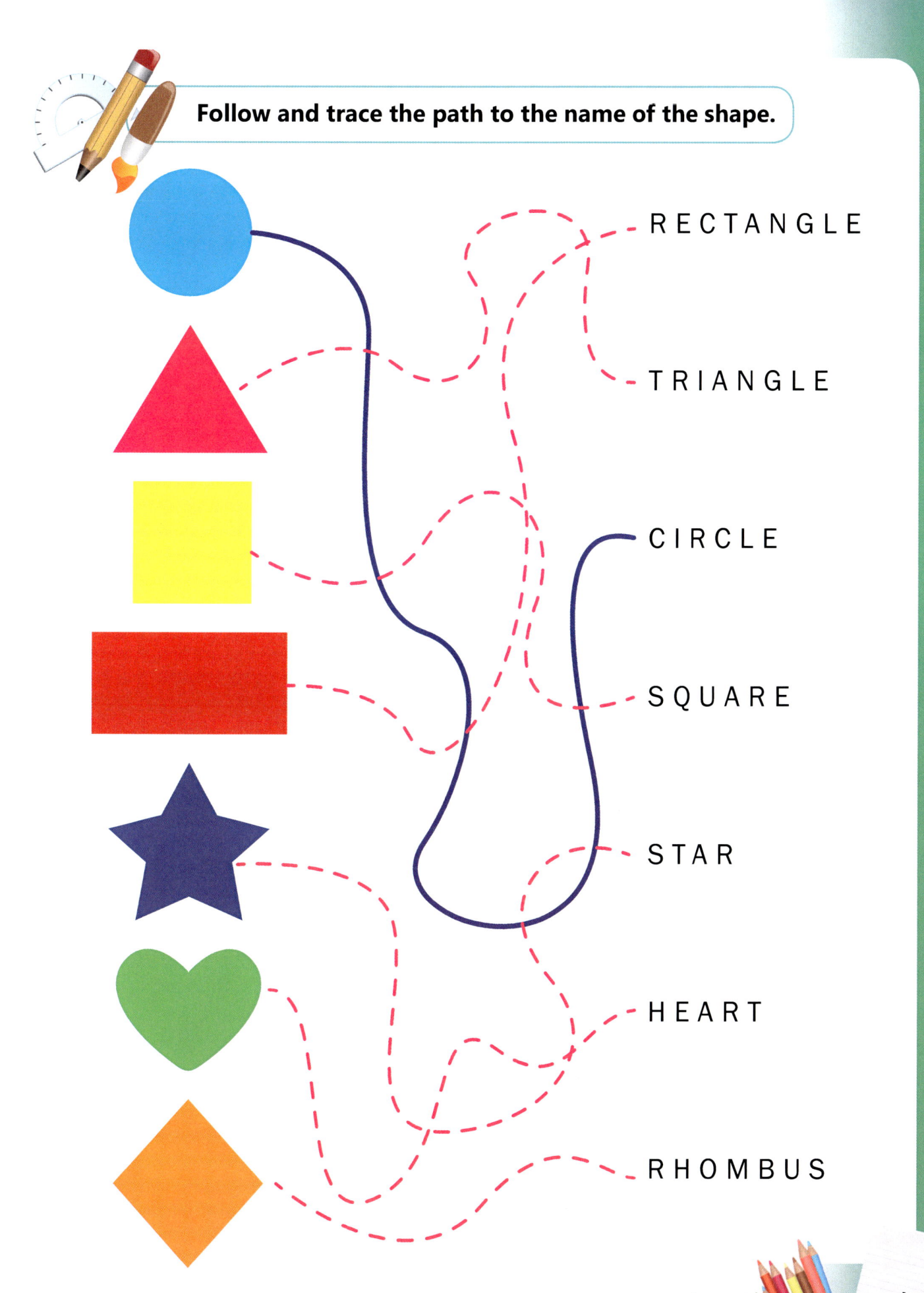

TRIANGLE

CIRCLE

SQUARE

STAR

HEART

RHOMBUS

43

Solve the puzzle and find the mystery word.

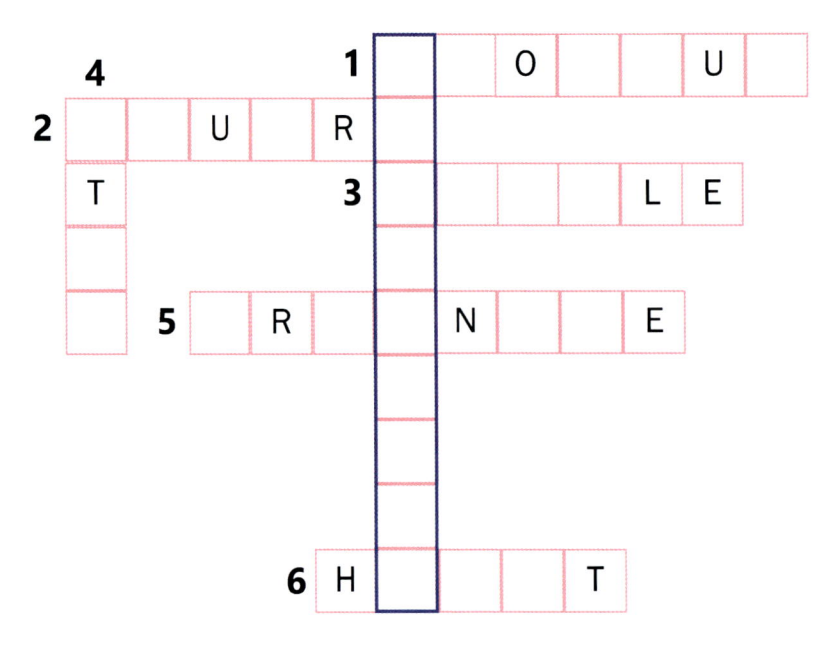

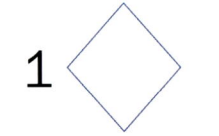

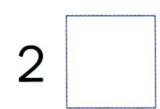

			4			1		O		U
2				U		R				
			T			3			L	E
		5		R			N		E	
						6	H		T	

1 ◇ 2 ☐ 3 ◯ 4 ☆ 5 △ 6 ♡

Draw the indicated shapes.

Heart   Triangle   Square

Star   Rectangle   Circle

Draw the indicated shapes.

Four triangles	Six rectangles	Two hearts
Three stars	Seven circles	Five squares

Match the objects with the shapes.

Find and circle the shapes in the picture

1. Three circles.
2. One triangle.
3. Five rectangles
4. Three squares

Farm animals

Look at the pictures and read.

Goose

Chick

Hen

Turkey

Rooster

Dog

Rabbit

Ox

Cat

Cow

Lamb

Goat

Pig

Sheep

Horse

Duck

48

Look at the pictures and repeat the sound of each animal.

Cat — meow

Dog — woof

Chick — chirp

Rooster — cockadoodledoo

Cow — moo

Pig — oink

Sheep — baa

Horse — neigh

49

Write the name of each animal.

1. _____Goat_____   3. _____   6. _____

2. _____   4. _____   7. _____

5. _____

50

Find the farm animals in the wordsquare.

Goose
Chick
Hen
Rooster
Turkey
Ox
Cat
Dog
Rabbit
Lamb
Goat
Pig
Cow
Sheep
Horse
Duck

T	Y	U	F	D	S	E	W	G	H	A	T	X	N
N	D	C	P	O	I	M	O	X	Q	H	C	O	W
F	G	H	D	W	G	N	M	S	H	Q	A	T	Y
L	P	I	Z	R	O	O	S	T	E	R	T	J	K
M	N	C	H	J	O	P	Q	V	N	R	E	R	H
K	L	K	N	M	S	K	L	P	H	V	N	A	J
G	T	U	R	K	E	Y	I	D	O	G	M	B	K
H	J	D	S	C	V	B	E	W	R	O	R	B	L
L	A	M	B	X	Z	K	J	U	S	A	T	I	Y
A	M	V	B	V	N	P	I	G	E	T	U	T	T
S	D	L	S	H	E	E	P	H	S	D	U	C	K
T	Y	E	N	M	Q	D	A	J	K	Y	U	E	R

Match the pictures with the correct animal.

Pig

Rabbit

Cow

Horse

Chick

Sheep

51

Fill in the missing letters of the animals.

C _ I _ K

P I _

H _ N

G _ O S _

C O _

R O _ S T _ R

C _ T

_ O G

H O _ S _

S _ E E _

52

Sources

DK. English for Everyone: Level 1: Beginner, Course Book: A Complete Self-Study Program. DK; Reprint edition. June 28, 2016.

Rafielle E. Usher. Yo Puedo! Speak English Now: ESL Libro de trabajo para aprender Ingles bilingue (Volume 1). O.M.I. International. January 27, 2014.

William C. Harvey M.S. Ingles para Latinos, Level 1. Barron's Educational Series; 3 edition. August 1, 2011.

Matthew Preston. Preston Lee's Beginner English Lesson 1 - 20 For Spanish Speakers. CreateSpace Independent Publishing Platform; Large Print edition. June 1, 2017.

J Lubandi. ENGLISH – SPANISH Picture Dictionary (INGLÉS - ESPAÑOL Diccionario de Imágenes). October 15, 2016.

Jonathan Crichton. English Made Easy Volume One: Learning English through Pictures. Tuttle Publishing. February 5, 2013.

Germaine Choe. English for Kids: 10 First Reader Books with Online Audio, Set 1 by Language Together. Language Together; 1st edition. 2016.

DK. Merriam-Webster Children's Dictionary: Features 3,000 Photographs and Illustrations. DK Children. May 19, 2015.

Miryung Pitts. ESL Worksheets and Activities for Kids. ECQ Publishing; 1 edition. October 15, 2014.

Roger Priddy. First 100 Words Bilingual: Primeras 100 palabras - Spanish-English Bilingual (Spanish Edition). Priddy Books; Bilingual edition. February 19, 2013.

Carol Vorderman. Help Your Kids with English. DK Publishing. 2013.

NEVER STO

LEARNING

Made in the USA
Las Vegas, NV
28 February 2024

86377644R00036